NOCH·STEHT·MANCH
ALTES·HAUS:VER-
EHRT·ALS·SEINES
WIRKENS·STAETTE

LUDWIG·VAN·BEETHOVEN

KEIN·NEUES·WARD
ERBAUT:WAS·NICHT
SEIN·LEB·DURCH-

HEILIGENSTADT

HEILIGENSTADT

NUSSDORF

MOEDLING

BADEN

MOEDLING

1827

1927

What in the World?

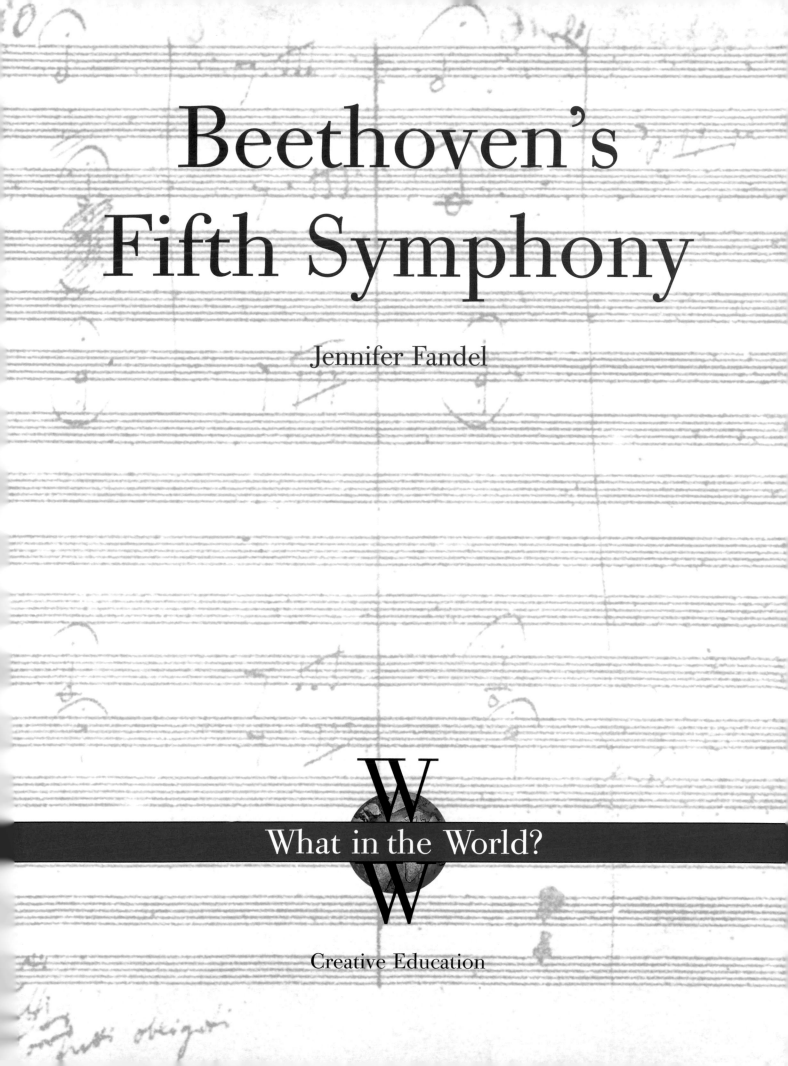

Beethoven's Fifth Symphony

Jennifer Fandel

What in the World?

Creative Education

Introduction

In his apartment strewn with freshly inked compositions, Ludwig van Beethoven scribbled notes fervently, afraid that his growing deafness would steal his music from him before he could put it to paper. His pen poised above the lined paper, he closed his eyes and listened to the music in his mind come alive. Like an unexpected knock at the door, the first four notes broke through the imagined silence. Moments later, the violins erupted again, boldly repeating the motif. Pouring his emotions into each note, the fiery composer created his Fifth Symphony, one of the most recognized and beloved pieces of music in all of history.

During World War II, Allied forces played a recording of the first four notes of Beethoven's Fifth Symphony as a signal of victory. Three short notes followed by one long one in Morse code stands for "V," or "Victory."

The rich, beautiful sound of the violin has long been important in orchestras.

Within the image:

LUDWIG VAN BEETHOVEN.

geb. 16. December 1770 zu Bonn,
+ 27. März 1827 zu Wien.

„FIDELIO."
„9 SYMPHONIEN." „MISSA SOLEMNIS."

LIEBIG COMPANY'S FLEISCH-EXTRACT.

Ludwig van Beethoven, widely regarded as one of the greatest composers of all time.

Like many Romantic artists, Englishman J.M.W. Turner, who painted Transept of Tintern Alley, *was captivated by nature.*

At the beginning of the 19th century, as Ludwig van Beethoven composed his Fifth Symphony, a spirit of change and a hope of new possibilities took hold around the world. In Europe, this spirit was the essence of the Romantic Movement.

Rebelling against the 18th century's devotion to logic and reason, the Romantics believed that emotions and imagination were the keys to a more fulfilling life. They considered rebels, adventurers, and artists to be the heroes of the age. Many of the Romantics, fascinated with folklore and exotic cultures, read and traveled widely. Some writers and artists, including English poet William Wordsworth, found inspiration exploring the countryside of England and Scotland, while others ventured into southern Europe, Africa, and Asia.

At the turn of the 19th century, people throughout Europe cultivated a sense of national identity through literature, art, and music. They revived many folk dances, such as Poland's mazurka and Scotland's schottische.

The mazurka is a lively dance with much stomping and heel clicking.

Men of the 19th century wore top hats for all occasions.

The expansion of trade also affected people's visions of the world. China opened its borders, which had been closed to foreigners for centuries. The shipments of tea, porcelains, and silks that sailed westward greatly affected European fashions, as furniture and tapestries began to be crafted in a Chinese style. Meanwhile, the small island of Singapore grew rapidly with immigrants from Europe, China, Thailand, Malaysia, and Java. As each culture erected its own mosques, churches, and temples, the trading port became known for its tolerant attitudes and ethnic diversity.

A London hatter made the first silk top hat in 1798. This reduced the need for American and Canadian beaver pelts, causing a rebound in the beaver populations of North America.

In the early 1800s, some European artists and writers turned to opium, a drug produced in Asia from poppies, to "free their minds." English poet Samuel Taylor Coleridge was said to have produced his famous poem "Kubla Khan" in a drug-induced state.

Poet Samuel Taylor Coleridge wrote about 13th-century Mongol leader Kublai Khan, whose armies are depicted here (opposite).

ازانجا پاى مرده درحده وشهر خوبكره وباورسيده وازانجانزول كرده ودرين مدت مكگونقاان محاصره قلعه مذكور مشعول بود وحكايت رنجور شدن نج
وفات يافتن ورسانيدن صندق وقل وراباورده وتعنيت داشتن موكگونقاان جون محاصره قلعه مذكور مى داديوقت انكه تابستان درآر
قوت كرفت آب وسوا انجا اسهال موى مىكرد وباد ميان لشكر مغول اث تاسپاى زنان مردنبا دپشاه جهان فح وباابشرب مىخورد وبران مداومت

VI

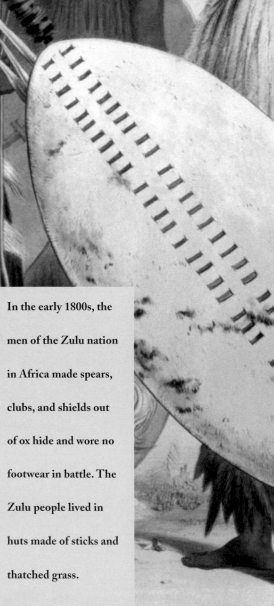

In the early 1800s, the men of the Zulu nation in Africa made spears, clubs, and shields out of ox hide and wore no footwear in battle. The Zulu people lived in huts made of sticks and thatched grass.

In 1799, the Rosetta Stone was discovered in Egypt. A stone tablet containing both ancient Egyptian hieroglyphics and Greek writing, the Rosetta Stone helped scholars decipher hieroglyphics, a language not yet understood at the time.

To the south, in Africa, Europeans began exploring and colonizing the continent's interior. While captivated by stories of mineral wealth and ample farmlands, many Europeans felt a mix of intrigue and worry as they moved into lands occupied by native Africans. The Zulu people in southeast Africa were led by a rebellious and ferocious leader named Shaka. Known for their skills as warriors, Zulu men brutally conquered surrounding tribes. Despite the growing influx of European settlers into southern Africa, the Zulu nation continued its powerful reign under Shaka for years and discouraged foreign settlement around its territories.

Across the Atlantic Ocean, in Central and South America, native peoples imagined their lives free from the Spanish colonial rule that had begun 300 years before. In Mexico, a priest named Miguel de Hidalgo inspired a successful peasant revolt in 1810. Stories of Hidalgo's success spread, fueling revolutions throughout Latin America for the next 15 years. In nearly every revolt, people were motivated by tales of fearless leaders such as Simon Bolivar, known as "The Liberator," who began campaigns for independence in Venezuela, Columbia, Ecuador, and Peru.

Zulu warriors (opposite) adorned with feathers; Egyptian hieroglyphics (above), which used pictures to represent words or sounds.

Francisco Goya painted his monumental The Third of May, 1808: Execution of the Defenders of Madrid *in 1814.*

A page from the Lewis and Clark expedition diary (above); a U. S. postage stamp honoring Johnny Appleseed (opposite).

In 1806, American Noah Webster began his work on *The American Dictionary of the English Language*. He learned 26 languages to find out the origins of words and included popular words heard only in the U.S.

In 1801, an American pioneer named John Chapman traveled from Pennsylvania to Ohio planting apple trees. Nicknamed "Johnny Appleseed," Chapman later returned to prune his saplings, helping the area become a rich source of apples.

To the north, the United States, fresh out of the American Revolution (1775-83), bought the Louisiana Territory from France, dramatically expanding the size of America. In 1804, explorers Meriwether Lewis and William Clark launched an expedition to survey the new lands west of the Mississippi River. Their bold mission captured the imagination of all Americans, for few knew what dangers and discoveries lay to the west. When the men returned to their starting point—the city of St. Louis—more than two years later, celebrations erupted across the country.

Meanwhile, the Romantic Movement grew in strength in Vienna, Austria, considered the musical capital and cultural heart of Europe. Known for its ornate concert halls, sprawling parks and gardens, and coffeehouses, Vienna prized the better things in life. There, music was taking a new direction, as composers broke away from musical styles of the past and created music that better reflected the changing emotions of the time. Many composers embraced the lengthy and complex symphony as the ultimate musical challenge.

In 1815, Dutchman Conrad J. Van Houten founded a chocolate factory in the Netherlands. Before this time, chocolate was a drink rather than a sweet confection.

Some of the most fashionable people in Europe promenaded along the boulevards of early 19th-century Vienna.

Coffeehouses were the places to meet old friends and enjoy life in Vienna. Beethoven and Franz Joseph Haydn often talked over coffee, hot chocolate, and tea. Fine pastries were also popular in these establishments.

For one young German pianist in particular, Vienna was a city of inspiration and promise. After the death of famed pianist and composer Wolfgang Amadeus Mozart in 1791, Ludwig van Beethoven aspired to become Vienna's new master composer. Straining against tradition and deafness, he would capture—in music—the emotions alive in all human struggles.

Wolfgang Amadeus Mozart (pictured) reputedly once said that Beethoven would "give the world something to talk about."

Seizing Fate

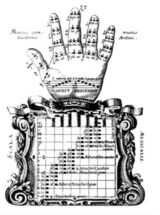

Ludwig van Beethoven was born on December 16, 1770, in Bonn, a small, prosperous town along the Rhine River in western Germany. The oldest of three sons born into a family of court musicians, Ludwig showed musical talent early. At age eight, Ludwig held his first public performance as a pianist. His father, Johann, wondered if he had a child prodigy like the great Mozart on his hands.

A withdrawn, sickly, but intense boy, Ludwig felt deeply connected to his music. Spending most of his time alone practicing the piano, he found making friends difficult. His

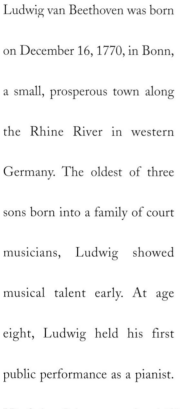

Beethoven substituted a slow, rhythmic dance, the minuet, with a lively movement, a scherzo, in the third movement, or part, of his Fifth Symphony. Later musicians viewed this as the standard symphonic form.

closest relationships were with his mother, Maria, and Christian Neefe, his music teacher and mentor. Under Neefe's guidance, Ludwig began composing songs, publishing his first at age 12.

Around this time, Ludwig also joined his father and grandfather as a court musician for the archbishop of Cologne. He began his career as an organist and, over the next five years, surpassed his fellow musicians in talent and skill. Recognizing this, they encouraged Ludwig to pursue a career beyond the comfortable streets of Bonn.

Beethoven's grandfather was among the musicians at this grand ball hosted by the archbishop of Cologne.

19

Magnificent churches and beautiful buildings were beginning to line the streets of Vienna in Beethoven's time.

Beethoven playing the piano for a group of admiring listeners, including Mozart, his teacher for a brief time.

WORDSWORTH.

English poet William Wordsworth published his collection *Lyrical Ballads* in the late 1700s. As a leader of the Romantic Movement, Wordsworth tried to capture the lives and the speech of common people.

In 1787, at age 17, Ludwig traveled for weeks by carriage west to Vienna, Austria, hoping to study under Mozart, who was then a well-established composer in his early 30s. While the composer praised Ludwig's dynamic improvisations during their brief time together, the young musician's opportunity with Mozart would be lost. Only weeks into his stay, Ludwig was called home. His mother, ill with tuberculosis, died soon after his arrival, and his father's once minor problems with alcohol worsened. Ludwig returned to his position in the court and began caring for his two younger brothers, Caspar and Nikolaus.

One of the most revered of the English poets, William Wordsworth saw beauty in the commonplace.

Composer Franz Joseph Haydn, wearing a traditional wig.

Beethoven, with his unruly natural hair.

In the beginning of the 19th century, men wore smaller wigs than had been common during the prior century and often tied them in a ponytail. Defying the conventions of the day, the rebellious Beethoven never wore a wig.

The symphony had developed only 100 years before Beethoven wrote his Fifth Symphony. At first, symphonies had only three movements. During Beethoven's time, they consisted of four movements and often took twice as long to perform.

Five years later, in 1792, a chance encounter with well-known composer Franz Joseph Haydn led 22-year-old Ludwig back to Vienna. Passing through Bonn, Haydn heard Ludwig's playing and convinced the archbishop to fund Ludwig's studies with the composer, as Mozart had died the year before. For a year, Ludwig met Haydn for regular practices and musical discussions in Vienna's many coffeehouses. Living in cramped attic lodgings, Ludwig longed to fit into his elegant surroundings, but his rough clothes, strong dialect, and gruff demeanor set the shaggy-haired young man apart.

A scene from Haydn's opera L'Incontro Improviso, *with the composer conducting at the front left of the orchestra.*

Beethoven's letter to his "Immortal Beloved," written in German, declares that "love demands everything."

Despite his difficulties adapting to Vienna's social scene, Ludwig quickly entered the spotlight and became known for his intelligence and charisma, as well as his stubborn and temperamental nature. Within two years, he rose to the status of master pianist through his performances at salons, informal gatherings held in people's homes. Working as a freelance musician, Ludwig supported himself through performances, publication of his compositions, and by teaching private music lessons.

During these years and throughout the composer's life, Ludwig's music lessons kindled many romances, as women of all ages were drawn to his passion for music. While he enjoyed these romances and, at times, fell deeply in love, he feared that a serious relationship would take him from his music. Yet he was never forced to choose. Nearly all of the women, from wealthy families and a higher standing than Ludwig, were out of his social class.

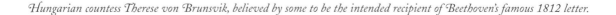

Hungarian countess Therese von Brunsvik, believed by some to be the intended recipient of Beethoven's famous 1812 letter.

Beethoven's patron, Prince Karl Lichnowsky.

As his musical reputation grew, Ludwig also enjoyed the friendship and financial support of Vienna's aristocrats, many of whom were willing to put up with Ludwig's flaring temper and biting words. While the young composer depended upon his patrons' generosity, he hated to feel controlled. In one instance, he dashed off a bitter letter to one of his most loyal patrons, Prince Karl Lichnowsky, writing, "There have been and will be thousands of princes; there is only one Beethoven."

In the late 1700s, many wealthy, young British men spent a few years on "The Grand Tour," an artistic and cultural excursion through Europe. With Rome, Italy, as their final destination, these aristocrats hoped to develop more sophisticated tastes through travel.

English chemist Humphry Davy discovered nitrous oxide, often called laughing gas, in 1799. He suggested its use as an anesthetic for minor surgery.

Vienna's Burgtheatre (opposite), founded in 1745, has been the venue for the premiere of works by numerous celebrated composers.

As Ludwig enjoyed increasing success and popularity, he strove to cement his reputation by composing symphonies and other longer works. Ludwig's first major public performance came in 1795, when he played a piano concerto at the Burgtheatre, one of the city's most prestigious music houses. In 1800, at age 30, he performed his First Symphony and immediately began work on his Second Symphony.

Ships laden with exotic exports such as tea and silk sailed from China to the West in the early 1800s.

In 1801, the Chinese city of Canton— a trading port for the United States, Britain, and the Netherlands— became, for a short time, the world's largest city, with a population of one and a half million people.

Beethoven used trombones in his Fifth Symphony. Before that time, the brass sections of orchestras typically included only trumpets and horns.

While bolstered by the strong public reception of his First Symphony, Ludwig confided to a friend a troubling secret. He was growing deaf and worried that it would end his career. For the next few years, gripped by feelings of despair and loneliness, he contemplated ending his life.

In 1802, as Ludwig wrote a suicide letter to his brothers, he came to a stunning realization. Despite his hearing loss, he still felt great joy in composing music. Tucking away the letter, Ludwig immersed himself in his work. Struggling against his fears, he wrote, "I will seize Fate by the throat; it will certainly not bend and crush me completely." In the spirit of these words, he imagined blazing trombones and fervent violins as they swelled the darkness with glorious sound.

Beethoven's use of the trombone influenced many later composers.

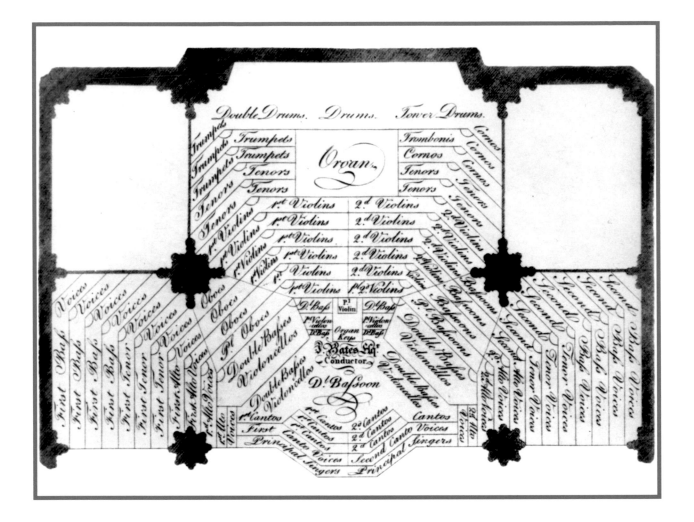

A typical orchestra in Beethoven's day consisted of 30 to 40 musicians, but occasionally a much larger orchestra was assembled.

One of the bound manuscripts in which Beethoven plotted the notes of his symphonies.

As his deafness worsened, Beethoven used an ear trumpet to converse. The ear trumpet, shaped like a megaphone, helped amplify sound. In later years, he asked guests to write their conversation in small books, which he read.

Beethoven's health was often poor, but he was most pained by his worsening deafness.

Beethoven was an artist of sound yet came to require an ear trumpet to receive sound himself.

By 1804, Ludwig's ability to hear was greatly diminished. Soft and high pitches were becoming imperceptible, and he had an increasingly difficult time conversing with others. Hoping to hide his deafness, he withdrew from society. To communicate with others, he poured his emotions—all of his hopes and worries—into the composition of his Fifth Symphony.

In 1801, French inventor Joseph Marie Jacquard created the automatic Jacquard loom. The loom helped weavers create designs within a fabric, greatly reducing the cost of patterned cloth.

On many days, Ludwig found inspiration for the symphony in Vienna's parks and gardens. He walked for hours, absorbed in the music playing inside his mind. He hummed and gestured wildly at times, and often talked to himself. Once full of new ideas, Ludwig would return home to continue his work.

An intricate pattern created on a Jacquard loom.

Gatherings at which Beethoven played the piano for his friends became less common as his deafness worsened.

Vienna's lush landscape provided abundant inspiration for Beethoven's creative genius.

To catalog the music of composers in libraries and publishing houses, compositions are assigned an opus number. Beethoven's famous symphony is formally written as Symphony No. 5 in C Minor, Op. 67.

Ludwig's apartment was in a state of constant chaos. Dust was thick on the mahogany grand piano, pens crusted with ink littered the tables, and chairs around the room held plates of half-eaten food. Always working on a number of projects at once, Ludwig was forever misplacing the loose leaves of his compositions among the clutter in his room. But opening his large bound sketchbook was like walking into a pristine chapel. On those oblong pages, Ludwig made sure every note was neatly recorded.

For four years, he worked out both the larger shape and the small details of his Fifth Symphony, carefully sketching out each melody.

Beethoven's disorganized apartment belied the harmony on the pages of his music.

In Ludwig's earliest symphonies, he had looked to Mozart and Haydn for inspiration, since their compositions had helped make symphonies, as a musical form, more popular. He closely followed their style, which emphasized controlling the music to please the ear. In Ludwig's Fifth Symphony, however, his impulses led him away from the techniques of his famous predecessors. Driven by his own wide-ranging emotions, Ludwig aimed to write a piece of music that, while still pleasing to the ear, did more to engage the heart. He finished his symphony in 1808.

In the early 1800s, Japan slowly opened its borders to trade and European ideas. New knowledge was spread through translations of European books in subjects such as medicine, science, economics, foreign policy, and military tactics.

Beethoven's elaborately decorated inkwell and the quills with which he wrote his music.

Firefly Hunting *by 19th-century Japanese artist Utagawa Kunisada, whose works influenced many Western artists.*

Deutsche Märchen in Wort und Bild.

2

Schneeweißchen.

Widmung.

Was wärst du schöne Jugendzeit
Denn ohne Märchenblüthen?
Wenn sie nicht goldnen Sternen gleich
An deinem Himmel glühten.

Ein Jugendmorgen ohne sie
Er wäre halbes Leben;
Du glücklich Kind, dem sie den Lenz
Der Jugend hold umschweben.

Gewiß man sagt es unbewußt:
„Das Märchen sei nur Lüge;"
Es ist des Kindes reinste Lust,
Des Kindergeistes Wiege.

Gedeih'! du ewig grüner Baum
Streu deinen Blüthensegen
Der goldnen Jugend in den Schooß
Wie einen Zauberregen.

Frankfurt am Main
Verlag von
E. G. May Söhne.

The Fifth Symphony, lasting around 30 minutes, opens with the most recognized four notes in all of music. Bold violins surge through the silence with a simple "bum-bum-bum-BUM," capturing listeners with their intensity. Then, moments later, the violins repeat the four-note motif, maintaining the same tense pressure. The music rushes headlong into conflict, the instruments quieting only for moments before raging again.

Throughout the first movement, Ludwig repeated the four-note motif often, using different instruments and altering the tempo to emphasize varied feelings, from fear to fleeting joy. While the motif is most noticeable in the first movement, he used it throughout the symphony to link the emotions of the different movements together.

Ludwig also stunned listeners by breaking away from tradition in his fourth and final movement. Most symphonies contain a pause between each movement. In the third movement of the Fifth Symphony, the violins' last notes climb higher and higher relentlessly, providing a bridge to the fourth movement and giving listeners no time to rest before bright horns explode into song.

The German title page to the Grimm brothers' fairy tale "Snow White."

The Theater an der Wien was unheated during Beethoven's December 1808 concert, causing the audience much discomfort.

On a bitterly cold night in December 1808, the Fifth Symphony made its debut at Vienna's Theater an der Wien, with Ludwig appearing as the orchestra's conductor that evening. The performance fell short of Ludwig's—and the audience's—expectations. The orchestra's poor playing caused Ludwig to stop the performance at one point, and listeners complained about the concert's length. Lasting more than four hours, the performance included Ludwig's Fifth and Sixth symphonies and many of his other latest works.

The first three movements of the Fifth Symphony are in the key of C minor. The harsh minor keys emphasize struggle. The last movement in C major conveys a happier tone, providing a sense of triumph over the earlier conflict.

In the late 19th century, scenes from Beethoven's opera Fidelio *were used in advertisements for meat extract.*

Although Beethoven was a prolific composer, with more than 840 musical creations, Fidelio *was his only opera.*

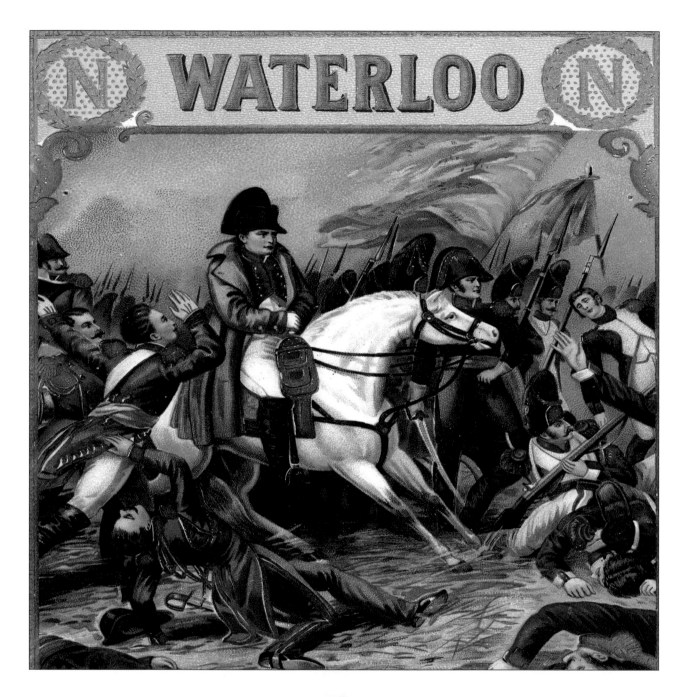

On June 18, 1815, the
battle of Waterloo was
fought between
Napoleon I's French
forces and an alliance
of Prussia (a former
state in northern
Europe), Russia,
Britain, and Austria.
The battle resulted in
defeat for Napoleon,
who was later exiled.

In 1813, German
musician Johann
Malzel invented the
metronome, a device to
keep tempo when play-
ing music. Beethoven
and others of the time
praised the invention.

Despite its poor debut, the Fifth Symphony quickly became recognized by music critics throughout Europe for its innovations and powerful emotion. Still, for 10 years after its first performance, the Fifth Symphony lived rather quietly, a piece of published music passed among conductors and musicians and described by critics in music magazines. Then, beginning around 1820, a number of concert halls in Vienna and throughout Europe performed the Fifth Symphony, making it a regular selection on their programs. It was around this same time that Ludwig's fame and musical genius spread across the Atlantic Ocean to North America.

In the years that immediately followed the Fifth Symphony's creation, a legend developed about the music. Ludwig, according to a critic, once commented on his four-note motif with the words, "Thus, fate knocks at the door." In later years, other critics elaborated on this idea, providing their own interpretations of the symphony and its connection to Ludwig's life. Fewer than 10 years after the symphony's debut, Ludwig made his now-complete deafness public, and the story of his struggle engaged the imagination of symphony aficionados and occasional listeners alike.

An illustration of Napoleon at the battle of Waterloo (opposite top); a metronome (opposite bottom).

Over the last two centuries, Ludwig van Beethoven, with his unrelenting gaze and wild hair, has become the embodiment of the Romantic artist—a rebel fueled by emotions. And while the Fifth Symphony is tightly bound to his life, the music has continued to live on its own for the emotional spell it casts on all who hear it.

Today, as in 1808, instruments and melodies weave together throughout the symphony in an intricate and complex tapestry of sounds and emotions. The violins brood, pulse, and lilt, their bows fast across the taut strings. The lonely, windy sound of the oboe lingers in momentary silence. The horns blare their crisp, emphatic sound. Then, in the symphony's final minute, all instruments boldly come together. Climbing higher and higher, they meet in eight powerful notes that press out doubt and darkness, resounding with joy.

On March 29, 1827, the day of Beethoven's funeral, 20,000 people turned out on Vienna's streets hoping to get a final look at the great man. The composer's large gravestone, just outside of Vienna, simply reads "Beethoven" in bold letters.

Voyager, a spacecraft launched toward deep space in 1977, is carrying the Golden Record, a collection of images, sounds, and music that best represent the cultures of Earth. Beethoven's Fifth Symphony is among the musical selections.

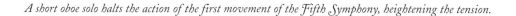

A short oboe solo halts the action of the first movement of the Fifth Symphony, heightening the tension.

Ludwig van Beethoven triumphed over adversity to create many of the greatest musical masterpieces the world has ever known.

What in the World?

1770	Ludwig van Beethoven is born in Bonn, Germany.
1778	Beethoven gives his first musical performance, in Cologne, Germany.
1781	The first iron bridge in the world is erected in England across the Severn River.
1782	Beethoven is appointed to his first musical position as court organist in Bonn.
1792	After leaving Bonn once to study with Mozart, Beethoven travels to Vienna, Austria, never to return.
1796	The first recipes for Native American dishes appear in an American cookbook.
1799	A woolly mammoth preserved in ice is discovered in Siberia by a native hunter.
1800	Beethoven composes his First Symphony.
1803	The world's first restaurant guide is published in France and lists more than 500 Parisian restaurants.
1808	Beethoven's Fifth Symphony debuts in Vienna.
1810	Germany's first Oktoberfest begins as a festival for the marriage of Bavaria's Prince Ludwig and Princess Therese.
1812	*Fairy Tales*, by German brothers Jakob and Wilhelm Grimm, is published.
1813	The London Philharmonic Society is founded to promote the performance and appreciation of music.
1815	An ailing and deaf Beethoven gives his last public performance on piano.
1819	The first successful transatlantic steamship crossing occurs between the United States and England.
1820	The 1,700-year-old statue *Venus de Milo* is discovered by a peasant in Greece.
1824	Beethoven completes the Ninth Symphony, his last.
1825	The Erie Canal opens, linking America's Great Lakes to the Hudson River and the Atlantic Ocean.
1827	Beethoven dies of liver disease in Vienna at the age of 56.

While Beethoven was transforming music, the Grimm brothers were making a mark on literature, and woolly mammoths were being uncovered.

Copyright

Published by Creative Education
123 South Broad Street, Mankato, Minnesota 56001

Creative Education is an imprint of The Creative Company.
Design by Rita Marshall
Production design by Melinda Belter

Photographs by Alamy (Peter Barritt, Classic Image IMAGEiN, Lebrecht Music and Arts Photo Library, The National Trust Photolibrary, North Wind Picture Archives, POPPERFOTO, JIM POWELL, V&A Images, Visual Arts Library (London)), Archive Photos, Art Resource, NY (Blidarchiv Preussischer Kulturbesitz, Werner Forman, Erich Lessing, Snark), Corbis (The Austrian Archives), Getty Images (George French Angas, Hulton Archive, Imango / Austrian Archives), The Bridgeman Art Library (Ludwig van Beethoven (1770–1827) Composing his 'Missa Solemnis,' 1819 (oil on canvas), Stieler, Joseph Carl (1781–1858) / Beethoven Haus, Bonn, Germany.) The Granger Collection, New York (page 20 bottom, page 25, page 34)

Illustrations: copyright © 2007 Etienne Delessert (cover, 1, 3, 46, 48), copyright © 2007 David Macaulay (46).

Library of Congress Cataloging-in-Publication Data
Fandel, Jennifer.
Beethoven's fifth symphony / by Jennifer Fandel.
p. cm. — (What in the world?)
ISBN 13: 978-1-58341-429-3
1. Beethoven, Ludwig van, 1770-1827. Symphonies, no. 5, op. 67, C minor—Juvenile literature. 2. Beethoven, Ludwig van, 1770-1827—Juvenile literature. I. Title. II. Series.

ML3930.B4F36 2006   784.2'184—dc22   2005050037

First Edition
9 8 7 6 5 4 3 2 1

Index